THIS IS
HOW WE
GOT HERE

ALSO BY KEITH BARKER

The Hours That Remain

THIS IS HOW WE GOT HERE

by keith barker

PLAYWRIGHTS CANADA PRESS
TORONTO

This Is How We Got Here © Copyright 2017 by Keith Barker

No part of this book may be reproduced, downloaded, or used in any form or by any means without the prior written permission of the publisher, except for excerpts in a review or by a licence from Access Copyright, www.accesscopyright.ca.

For professional or amateur production rights, please contact Playwrights Canada Press.

LIBRARY AND ARCHIVES CANADA CATALOGUING IN PUBLICATION
Barker, Keith (Keith Norman Victor), author
    This is how we got here / Keith Barker. -- First edition.

A play.
Issued in print and electronic formats.
ISBN 978-1-77091-822-1 (softcover).--ISBN 978-1-77091-823-8 (PDF).--
ISBN 978-1-77091-824-5 (EPUB).--ISBN 978-1-77091-825-2 (Kindle)

    I. Title.

PS8603.A73556T45 2017   C812'.6   C2017-906066-X
                                               C2017-906067-8

Playwrights Canada Press operates on Mississaugas of the Credit, Wendat, Anishinaabe, Métis, and Haudenosaunee land. It always was and always will be Indigenous land.

We acknowledge the financial support of the Canada Council for the Arts—which last year invested $153 million to bring the arts to Canadians throughout the country—the Ontario Arts Council (OAC), Ontario Creates, and the Government of Canada for our publishing activities.

Canada Council for the Arts / Conseil des arts du Canada

ONTARIO ARTS COUNCIL
CONSEIL DES ARTS DE L'ONTARIO
an Ontario government agency
un organisme du gouvernement de l'Ontario

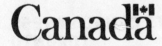
Canada

Ontario
Ontario Media Development Corporation

For Aaron, Craig, Daniel, and Carol.

This Is How We Got Here was first produced by Theatre Continuum and New Harlem Productions as part of the SummerWorks Performance Festival at Factory Theatre, Toronto, from August 4 to 14, 2016, with the following cast and creative team:

Lucille: Peggy Coffey
Paul: James Downing
Liset: Deborah Drakeford
Jim: Martin Julien
Voice-over: Marc Blanchard

Director: Eli Ham
Set Design: Ryan Howard Clement
Artwork and Graphic Design: Travis Murphy
Fox Prop: Deb Erb
Costume Design: Isidra Cruz
Sound Design and Live Performance: Deanna Choi
Lighting Consultant: Wendy Greenwood

He gave one last long look across the sky, across that magnificent silver land where he had learned so much.

"I'm ready," he said at last. And Jonathan Livingstone Seagull rose with the two starbright gulls to disappear into a perfect dark sky.

—Richard Bach, *Jonathan Livingston Seagull*

CHARACTERS

Paul: Craig's father, Lucille's husband, and Jim's best friend.
Lucille: Craig's mother, Paul's wife, and Liset's sister.
Liset: Lucille's sister, Craig's aunt, and Jim's wife.
Jim: Liset's husband, Craig's uncle, and Paul's best friend.

Please note the character of Craig is revealed in a voice recording at the end of the play.

SCENE 1—ONE-YEAR ANNIVERSARY

JIM walks in dressed up for the cold. He carries a flashlight. He stops and looks around. PAUL enters dressed much the same.

JIM   So? Where should we start?

PAUL   Depends. Which way did she go?

JIM   That way or was it? No. No, she went that way.

JIM starts to walk in the direction he indicated.

PAUL   Where you going?

JIM   She went that way.

PAUL   Yeah, but the creek runs that way. Which means she probably followed it down past George's and over—

JIM   —to Harland's. Good thinking.

JIM starts to walk towards Harland's.

PAUL   Now where you going?

JIM   You just said Harland's.

PAUL   Yeah, but there's nothing past Harland's except the lake.
        Which means she probably headed north along the hydro
        lines to Carol's Creek.

JIM   You really think she'd go that far?

PAUL   Only one way to find out.

Both men exit in opposite directions.

        This way.

JIM immediately adjusts his mistake and follows PAUL.

JIM   Right, this way.

SCENE 2—FOX STORY PART 1

PAUL   Once there was a fox who lived in the forest and he had
a magical gift for storytelling. Animals would come from
all around and from far away just to hear his stories. And
the fox would spend all of his days making up story after
story and telling them to anyone who would listen. But
one day, as sometimes happens, things changed, and the
fox—when asked by the badger to tell his own story—
could not remember it. In fact, he could not remember
any of his own stories. It seems he had told so many stories
to so many people that he had, in fact, lost his own. This
worried the fox. He had never lost his own story before.
It had always been there to tell him which way to go and
what to do next. But now it was gone and he felt very alone.
Luckily he still had the story of today, and today, like all
the days before it, had been good. But today was quickly
coming to an end. And if today ended before he could find
his story again, what would that mean for tomorrow? With
no story there would be no tomorrow. What was he going
to do?

SCENE 3—ONE-YEAR ANNIVERSARY

LISET and JIM's house. PAUL is waiting at the door. He knocks and waits the appropriate amount of time one does when waiting for someone to answer. Then he starts to leave. LISET opens the door.

LISET   Paul? Is that you?

PAUL   Oh hey, Liz, how's it going?

LISET   Good, and you?

PAUL   Oh you know, it goes.

LISET   Yeah.

Beat.

           I'm sorry but we have to make this quick—I'm in the middle of making dinner.

PAUL   I don't mean to interrupt—

LISET   You didn't. What's up?

Beat.

PAUL   Liz, I know things haven't been good between us lately.

LISET   Uh huh.

PAUL   But I was just wondering if maybe we could put our differences aside for one night so I could see Lucille.

LISET   Seriously, that's what you're here for?

PAUL   Listen—

LISET   No, you listen to me. She made it very clear she doesn't want to see you.

PAUL   A couple of minutes is all I'm asking for.

LISET   I'm sorry.

PAUL   If she says no I'll go away, I promise.

LISET   She doesn't want to see you.

PAUL   Just go in there and ask her, would ya?

LISET   I'm not doing that!

PAUL   WHY NOT? Am I that terrible of a person that you won't even let me see my wife on the anniversary?

She holds her ground.

You are unbelievable; you really are.

PAUL walks away.

LISET WAIT . . . She's been . . . struggling. With you two and the divorce it's only made things worse. She spends most of her days outside in the backyard. She doesn't talk; she doesn't want to talk; she barely eats; and I know she's not sleeping. Mostly she wants to be left alone, so that's what I try to do: I try to leave her alone. Some days are better than others. Today is not one of those days. She's fragile and I'm afraid if she sees you it's gonna . . . you know—

PAUL Yeah.

Beat.

LISET Anyways I've got to get back inside, dinner is on the stove.

PAUL Yeah, no, of course. I'll get out of your way.

PAUL *goes to leave.*

LISET Listen . . . I'll tell her you stopped by. If she wants to see you I will drive her over. Deal?

PAUL Deal.

SCENE 4—TWO WEEKS BEFORE THE ANNIVERSARY

PAUL and LUCILLE's house. We hear the sound of a pick-up truck pulling up. A truck door opens and closes. After a moment:

JIM   *(from off)* Paul? You home?

PAUL   *(from off)* In here!

After a moment JIM enters. He has a slight limp due to a sore back and his hand is bandaged up. PAUL enters shortly after.

             What's up?

JIM   Not much. Whatcha up to?

PAUL   Working on the well. I keep getting sediment in the water.

JIM   Oh, that's not good.

PAUL   Yeah well, hopefully I can patch it 'cause I can't afford to drill a new one.

    Beat.

JIM   So, you gonna offer me a drink or what?

PAUL   Since when do you ask? Help yourself to whatever's in the fridge. I got juice in there somewheres.

JIM   Juice?

PAUL   Yeah, juice.

JIM   What kind of juice?

PAUL   I don't know, does it matter?

JIM   Guess not. You got anything else?

PAUL   Like what?

JIM   Like, I don't know, you got any beer?

PAUL   No, but I got some pop in the fridge downstairs. Give me a sec—

JIM   Nah don't worry about it.

PAUL   You sure?

JIM   Yeah, no, I'm fine.

PAUL   Suit yourself . . . So, what brings you over to this side of town?

JIM   I thought I'd return your Shop-Vac to you.

PAUL   You came all the way over here for that?

JIM   Yeah well Liz has been nagging me about it for a while now. Hey, you got a light?

PAUL   Yeah, I got some matches, but you can't smoke in the house.

JIM   Since when?

PAUL   Since I've been trying to quit. But you can smoke on the porch if you like.

JIM   Uh, sure, sounds good.

JIM makes his way towards the door.

PAUL   What's up? Why are you limping like that?

JIM   Ah, it's my back—it's killing me. I've been sleeping on the couch the last few nights.

PAUL   Oh yeah?

JIM   Yeah.

PAUL   What'd you do?

JIM   Nothing.

PAUL   Nothing?

JIM   That's what I said.

PAUL   I know that's what you said, but you must have done something.

JIM   What's that supposed to mean?

PAUL   Nothing, what's wrong with your hand?

JIM Ah, just a dumb thing I did at work . . . Hey, I know we haven't, you know . . . seen a lot of each other since the uh—

PAUL Yeah, no, it's fine.

JIM I've been super busy at work—

PAUL Yeah me too. Here let me grab you those matches.

JIM Sure . . .

PAUL *goes off.*

. . . Hey, you get any moose this year?

PAUL No, you?

JIM Yeah, I got a bull. Dale got one too.

PAUL Oh yeah? I totally forgot this year.

JIM You should put your name in with the police. They'll call you if someone hits one on the highway.

PAUL *re-enters.*

PAUL Yeah, I thought about it, but it kind of feels like I'm cheating, you know what I mean?

JIM Yeah, but a moose is a moose, right?

PAUL Right.

JIM   As long as you don't mind spitting out a bit of glass at the dinner table.

This breaks the tension.

        Hey, you remember the time Dale hit that moose driving back from the Peg.

PAUL   Like it was yesterday. I totally thought we were going to die that night.

JIM   Oh, me too.

PAUL   One second we're talking and laughing, and the next second there's a moose coming through the front window.

JIM   Oh man, we were lucky we only hit the back end of her.

PAUL   Yeah, I know.

JIM   Counted my lucky stars that night.

PAUL   Oh me too, and then Dale jumps out of the car and starts yelling at the poor thing.

JIM   Which was fine until she stood up.

PAUL   Oh man, the look on his face as he was running back to the car.

JIM   *(mimics Dale)* "Open the door, open the door!"

PAUL   Barely got it open in time.

JIM   When she charged the car like that I thought we were
             done for.

PAUL   And then Eric—

JIM   Oh man! The only guy in the car who hates hunting—

PAUL   Ends up shooting the moose—

JIM   From the back seat of the car!

PAUL   Who does that?

JIM   A dentist, that's who. My ears were ringing for a week.

PAUL   Mine too.

JIM   Still don't know how we managed to get her home that night.

PAUL   Worst idea ever.

JIM   It's the only time in my life where I've driven home with
             four hundred pounds of moose in my lap and another five
             hundred strapped to the roof.

PAUL   Tied down with duct tape and extension cords. And the
             smell?

JIM   Jee-sus. I can still remember Barb's face when we pulled
             up to the house.

PAUL   That's 'cause it was her car!

JIM   And then you trying to convince Craig that we killed it in
             self-defence.

PAUL Almost worked too.

JIM Sorry, man.

PAUL For what?

JIM I didn't mean to . . . bring him up.

PAUL Don't be, it's a good story. Funny, Loo always said that's what made him a vegetarian.

JIM Yeah, who knows, eh? What is that?

PAUL What? Oh it's a chess set.

JIM I didn't know you played chess.

PAUL I don't. Well, not yet.

JIM What do you mean?

  PAUL sighs.

PAUL I met this guy at my support group. His son died a few years back so we got talking about the boys. He told me he'd signed up for some kayak lessons because it was something his son loved doing when he was alive. Said it helped him with the uh . . . Anyways Craig loved chess so I thought I would give it a try.

JIM Yeah, well, I've heard it's a good game. It's like advanced checkers.

PAUL Well, no, not really.

JIM   Same idea though but with different rules.

PAUL   And different pieces.

JIM   Exactly.

PAUL   So it's a completely different game.

JIM   Well, if you're going to be like that about it, then forget it.

PAUL   Forget what?

JIM   Hey, was that your truck parked outside of Benjamin Hurley's house a couple weeks ago?

PAUL   Uh, yeah. He was putting in a sauna, asked me to do the wiring for him.

JIM   Oh yeah?

PAUL   Yeah. He also needed some help laying the concrete in the basement.

JIM   Oh, so you were out there a lot.

PAUL   Well, not a lot—

JIM   Sounds like a lot.

PAUL   Well it wasn't.

JIM   You know he's a fruit, eh?

PAUL   He's not a fruit.

JIM   Yes he is.

PAUL   And what makes you so sure?

JIM   You've seen his hair, right?

PAUL   That doesn't mean anything.

JIM   He's a kindergarten teacher.

PAUL   Well I'm telling you, I spent a couple days with the guy and nothing like that is going on over there.

JIM   Oh yeah? And what makes you so sure?

PAUL   Trust me, I'm sure.

JIM   The guy teaches cooking classes out of his house, he has a cat, he drinks wine when he's at the bar, and he's got an orange car.

PAUL   Jerry's car is turquoise, you think he's a fruit?

JIM   No, because we all know Jerry's wife chose that colour.

PAUL   So?

JIM   So this guy doesn't have a wife!

PAUL   It's a stupid rumour.

JIM   Well a couple of the guys at the mill say it's not.

PAUL   And you listen to them?

JIM   They say he's from Montreal.

PAUL   So what?

JIM   And he drinks bottled water.

PAUL   I drink bottled water, what does that make me?

JIM   Don't do that!

PAUL   I'm serious!

JIM   So am I! *(under his breath)* . . . Fruit.

PAUL   Excuse me?

JIM   What?

PAUL   You calling me a fruit?

JIM   No.

PAUL   You just said fruit!

JIM   Yeah, but I said fruit like HE'S a fruit, not YOU'RE a fruit.

PAUL   That's not what you said!

JIM   Well, that's what I meant.

PAUL   I'm not a fruit.

JIM   I know.

PAUL   You've known me my whole life. You know me.

JIM   I know.

PAUL   If the boys start thinking I'm a fruit they're gonna start thinking you're a fruit too, you know what I mean?

JIM   No. What are you talking about?

PAUL   We've been best friends our whole lives.

JIM   I'm not a fruit!

PAUL   I didn't say you were.

JIM   Then why are you calling me a fruit?

PAUL   I wasn't calling you a fruit!

JIM   That's what you said!

PAUL   But that's not what I meant! What I was trying to say—

JIM   I don't care what you were trying to say, don't call me a fruit.

PAUL   You're not a fruit, I'm not a fruit, neither one of us are fruit, OKAY?

JIM   OKAY!

PAUL   Besides, there's nothing wrong with people like that. I'm just not one of them.

JIM   Yeah, well, I don't care for people like that.

PAUL   Yeah well I don't care for vegetarians, but I still talk to your wife.

JIM   That's different.

PAUL   Not in my eyes it's not.

JIM   Well it is in mine.

PAUL   And why is that?

JIM   You know why.

PAUL   Then say it.

JIM   No.

PAUL   Why not?

JIM   'Cause I don't want to.

PAUL   You can't, can you.

JIM   Would you drop it already?

PAUL   I'll drop it when you say it.

JIM   You say it.

PAUL   Coward.

JIM   Don't call me that.

PAUL   Then say it.

JIM   Because being gay is a sin! There!

PAUL   And what about suicide?

JIM   Ah, man . . . you know that's different.

PAUL   How?

JIM   It just is.

PAUL   Oh yeah? Then why do you still go to the same church
           that refused to have my son's funeral.

JIM   Oh come on. I've been going there my whole life.

PAUL   Yeah, well, if it's different then why didn't you say some-
           thing to Father Bob about it?

JIM   And what was I supposed to say?

PAUL   That he was a good kid. That he deserved to be buried with
           his family—my parents are buried there, Loo's parents are
           there too, but Craig isn't. He took away my son's last rights,
           so don't you go telling me it's different 'cause it's not.

JIM   Father Bob was just following the rules—

PAUL   If it's about the rules then why did Father David allow
           him to be buried at St. John's?

JIM   Father David comes from a different generation than
           Father Bob.

PAUL   I don't care! He humiliated us in front of everyone we
           know and I will never forgive him for that.

JIM   Paul, listen—

PAUL   No, I'm done listening.

PAUL *goes to leave.*

JIM   Where you going?

PAUL   I got to finish the well before it gets dark. You know the
           way out.

PAUL *exits.*

SCENE 5—ONE-YEAR ANNIVERSARY

LUCILLE is holding an egg wrapped in tissue. You can tell it is very dear to her.

LUCILLE   The day you were born was not the best day of my life. It was not the first time I ever saw your father cry and you were not the most precious thing we had ever seen. And I was never one of those annoying mothers who would talk endlessly about how great their child was. I did not gush about all the things you had done and all the things you were going to accomplish and I never once pulled out my wallet full of pictures to prove it. You didn't make me the best presents on my birthday and at Christmas, or leave me notes telling me how much you loved me. You never hugged and kissed me every night before bed no matter what, and you never wanted to curl up beside me on the couch on movie night. I never went to your hockey games and I didn't embarrass you by screaming my head off every time you touched the puck. We never had the awkward sex talk, and you didn't make fun of me about it for years after. I never caught you smoking cigarettes behind the house because you wanted to be more like your dad, and we didn't cry together that time Kelli broke your heart. We never used to talk late into the night with cinnamon toast and tea, or sing Billy Joel songs at the top of our lungs as we made homemade candy at Christmas. You were not gentle or sensitive or a romantic at heart. You were not the one thing I was most proud of in this world and you were not the part of me that I loved best. I was not your mother. I can't be. Because if I was . . . I wouldn't be able to go on from here.

LUCILLE's sister LISET comes out to the garden.

LISET   Hey, time for dinner. I'm grabbing veggies for the salad and then we're all sitting down to eat together. And NO is not an option tonight.

LISET sees that her vegetable garden is ruined. She is horrified.

Oh my God I'm gonna kill him, I really am.

Yelling to JIM off stage.

JIM, WE HAVE NO VEGGIES TONIGHT BECAUSE YOU DIDN'T BUILD A FENCE LIKE I ASKED YOU TO! NOW WHO'S PARANOID? Oh no, not my tomato plants, my carrots too, even my lettuce is gone. Oh come on now, really? The potatoes? What kind of animal digs up and eats potatoes?

LISET sees the fox. She turns and makes a break for the fox but LUCILLE stops her.

YOU! WHY YOU LITTLE SON OF A— You listen to me and you listen good, you little terror! If I catch you anywhere near my garden again I will kill you!

LUCILLE   Liz!

LISET   No, I'm serious! There is a rifle in my garage with your name on it!

LUCILLE   You wouldn't shoot a fox, would you?

LISET   God no, I'd get Jim to do it.

LUCILLE   Liz!

LISET   Look what it did!

LUCILLE   It's just a garden!

LISET   Yeah, but it's my garden and now it's ruined. What is that?

LUCILLE   What?

LISET   That. Right there.

LUCILLE   Nothing.

LISET   Well obviously it's something 'cause I can see it.

LUCILLE   You don't have to worry about it.

LISET   I'm not worried about it; I just want to know what it is.

LUCILLE   Well I don't want to tell you what it is.

LISET   Why not?

LUCILLE   Because I don't need a lecture right now.

LISET   I am not in the mood for this.

LUCILLE   Neither am I, so let's drop it.

LISET   If you don't tell me what it is right now, I will wrestle you
             to the ground and take it from you.

LUCILLE   You wouldn't.

LISET   Oh, I would. I'll give you to the count of three. One. I'm
             serious . . . Two . . . really? We're going to do this? Fine.
             THREE—

LISET makes a break for her but LUCILLE stops her.

LUCILLE   —don't don't don't. It's an egg, okay? It's an egg.

LISET   An egg?

LUCILLE   Yes.

LISET   Why do you have an egg?

LUCILLE   Because it's a long story and I don't want to talk about it.

LISET   And I take it this egg is not from the grocery store.

LUCILLE   No.

LISET   And what is so special about it?

LUCILLE   That's what I don't want to talk about.

LISET   Well you can't bring it into the house if that's what you
             were thinking. What? Birds carry all kinds of diseases we
             don't even know about. The best thing you can do right
             now is go put the egg back where it came from.

LUCILLE   I don't know where it came from.

LISET   Well I'm sure if you go back to where you found it and look up you'll discover something new and exciting.

LUCILLE   I didn't find it. It was given to me.

Beat.

LISET   Sometimes I wonder why I married him—JIM, GET OUT HERE NOW—

LUCILLE   It wasn't Jim, it was the fox!

LISET   The what?

LUCILLE   Nothing.

LISET   No, you need to explain what you just said.

Beat.

LUCILLE   Fine. But only if you promise me you'll listen to the whole story without interrupting me.

LISET   Sure . . . What? I promise.

Beat.

LUCILLE   When I came outside this morning the fox was out here waiting for me.

LISET   How do you know it was waiting for you?

LUCILLE   That's an interruption.

LISET   Right, sorry.

LUCILLE	He walked right up to me and he placed the egg at my feet. Then he ran away.
LISET	Maybe he was saving it for later.
LUCILLE	No, he wanted me to have it.
LISET	How do you know that?
LUCILLE	I just do.
LISET	So let me get this straight. You're holding an egg that was inside the mouth of a wild animal. When's the last time you washed your hands?
LUCILLE	That's not the point.
LISET	It is when you live in my house and you touch my stuff.
LUCILLE	Yes . . . from Craig.
LISET	Oh, don't do that.
LUCILLE	What?
LISET	That. What you're doing there, you can't do that. The egg is just an egg. There is no meaning behind any of it, so please don't start looking for something that isn't there. I know you're sad; I'm sad too, that's why I made dinner.
LUCILLE	I don't want dinner.
LISET	You know what? You're right. Forget it. Forget that I was trying to help, forget that I just spent three hours in the kitchen making something no one wants to eat. Forget that

Jim wants to stay out in the garage, and you'd rather be out here, and forget the fact that no one wants to talk to me, except for Paul of course, who shows up out of the blue and wants to see you, and I'm the one that has to say no. I know it's the anniversary, and I know it's hard, and I should be better about this, but I'm not. I'm pissed off, and this is not an excuse, it's not, but I haven't eaten all day and you know how I am when I haven't eaten. You're my little sister and I love you and I tried my best but it's just not working and everything I do is just, I don't know, give me a hug.

They hug.

LUCILLE   Paul was here?

LISET   Yeah. I sent him away.

LUCILLE   How is he doing?

LISET   Oh you know . . . he looked like a lost puppy. Last week I made Jim go over there to check in on him. I thought it would be good for the both of them but apparently it wasn't. I'm telling you those two guys are as stubborn as their fathers were.

LUCILLE   What do you mean?

LISET   Well, Jim said they ended up fighting over some fruit and then he left.

LUCILLE   That's weird. Paul doesn't even like fruit. I could barely get him to eat vegetables.

LISET   Hey, I'm as confused as you are.

LUCILLE   That's too bad. You can tell how much they miss each other.

LISET   I know. Anyways . . . If you want to see him today I can
             drive you over.

LUCILLE   I don't know.

LISET   No pressure.

LUCILLE   Thanks. Can you do me a favour?

LISET   Anything.

LUCILLE   Promise me you won't shoot the fox.

LISET   I promise . . . but only if you will come in for dinner . . .

They share a smile.

LUCILLE   Deal.

LISET   YOU HEAR THAT? THE GARDEN IS ALL YOURS!

She hugs her sister and heads inside.

SCENE 6—ONE-YEAR ANNIVERSARY

JIM enters with a flashlight and walks around looking for LUCILLE. With the light he finds a footprint. He stands looking at it.

JIM   Hey, I found something.

PAUL   *(off)* What?

JIM   Just get over here.

PAUL walks over to JIM and looks down.

PAUL   Tracks.

JIM   Yep. Looks like they go that way.

PAUL starts to walk back the way he came.

             Where you going? Shouldn't we follow these?

PAUL   No, probably not. Loo doesn't wear a size ten. But you do.

JIM   Those aren't size—oh yeah, maybe they are. Now what?

PAUL   Well . . . I say we still check Carol's Creek and then walk the hydro lines up to the quarry.

JIM   And if she's not there?

PAUL   Then we keep looking.

They exit.

SCENE 7—FOX STORY PART 2

LISET   The fox could see the day was coming to an end as the sun began to set. He needed to find his story and find it fast. First he tried doing what he did best—he told a made-up story about tomorrow and all the things he imagined would happen. But made-up stories are not real stories, so it did not work and the sun continued to set. Then he tried to find clues in all the memories of his life, but that didn't work either. Memories sent him in the wrong direction: to yesterday and days before, instead of to tomorrow and the days after that. And the long shadows of the afternoon appeared and the sun continued to set.

SCENE 8—ONE MONTH BEFORE THE ANNIVERSARY

LISET is pacing as she waits for JIM. She hears him outside and sits. JIM comes in from work.

LISET   What did I say about walking in here with your work boots on?

JIM   I'm hanging up my coat.

LISET   And I thank you for that, but take your boots off first.

JIM   I can't take them off when I've got my coat on.

LISET   Why not?

JIM   'Cause I can't!

LISET   Well you're not walking through here unless you take them off!

JIM   Oh, come on!

LISET   Jim, so help me God—

JIM   All right, all right, keep your panties on, I'm doing it.

LISET   Excuse me?

JIM   What? I said I'm doing it.

LISET   No, I warned you about that kind of language— You keep
             it at the mill or with your buddies, you got it?

JIM   Sorry.

LISET   —I'm your wife—

JIM   —I said I was sorry, all right?

LISET   All right . . . There's a towel hanging in the bathroom for
             you. Put your work clothes in the washing machine, NOT
             in the clothes hamper, got it?

JIM   Why do we have a clothes hamper if I can't put my clothes
             in it?

LISET   Can you do what I ask for once without all the hoopla?

JIM   The what?

LISET   Forget it, just put them in the washing machine!

JIM   Okay, I'm doing it. But only because I love you.

LISET   Yeah, well . . . thanks for that.

    JIM exits.

JIM   *(off)* Hey, what's for dinner?

LISET   Whatever you want. The fridge is full of options.

JIM   *(off)* You didn't make anything?

LISET I didn't say that.

JIM (*off*) Oh, so you made something, just not for me.

LISET Jim, I asked you this morning if you were going to be home for dinner and you said no.

JIM (*off*) Yeah, but I figured you'd still be making something.

LISET You're right, I did, and then I ate it.

JIM (*off*) Well, what am I supposed to do now?

LISET I don't know, you're a big boy, I'm sure you'll figure it out.

   JIM re-enters.

JIM Hey, is something wrong?

LISET No.

JIM Liz—

LISET I'm not making you dinner.

JIM I'm not asking you to.

LISET Good 'cause I'm not doing it.

JIM What's wrong?

LISET Nothing.

   JIM exits in frustration.

JIM   *(off)* Can you just tell me what it is so I can stop being punished for it.

LISET   I'm not punishing you for anything.

Beat. After a moment JIM *enters still wearing his coat. He goes to grab his boots.*

             What did I say about your work clothes?

He grabs them and starts to walk off.

JIM   Give me a second, would you? You were distracting me with your talking.

JIM *exits.*

LISET   Oh, I'm sorry, I thought we were having a conversation here.

JIM   *(off)* Where do you want 'em again?

LISET   I already told you this—in the washing machine. Not beside it, not on top of it, but IN it. It's really easy, you just lift the lid.

JIM   *(off)* Hey, don't talk to me like I'm a child.

LISET   Then don't act like one.

JIM   *(off)* Why are you being like that?

LISET   Because I love you.

JIM   *(off)* Right, well . . . thanks for that.

Beat.

LISET	You want me to zap you some of that chicken from last night?
JIM	*(off)* Nah. I had it for lunch. I'll grab something else.
LISET	Just so you know, I spoke with Lucille. She's going to come and stay with us for a while.
JIM	Oh. Why?
LISET	They got into a big fight again last night.

JIM enters eating a bowl of cereal.

JIM	Is everything all right?
LISET	I don't think so. He said some pretty terrible things. She's talking about leaving him.
JIM	No, really?
LISET	Yeah. What are you doing?
JIM	Nothing.
LISET	What is that?
JIM	Cereal.
LISET	You're having cereal for dinner?
JIM	Yeah, so?

LISET   Jim, that's not dinner.

JIM   Well it is tonight.

LISET   Are you trying to piss me off?

JIM   No.

LISET   'Cause if that's what you're trying to do, it's working.

JIM   I'm not.

LISET   Cereal? We have a fridge full of food and you're eating cereal.

JIM   Liset, are you going to tell me what's wrong or are we going to keep doing this all night?

LISET   There is nothing wrong.

JIM   Fine then, but let the record show that I did ask—MANY TIMES—what was wrong.

JIM exits.

LISET   You really want to know?

JIM   *(off)* Oh, so I did do something wrong.

LISET   Do you want to know or not?

He re-enters, going to her immediately.

JIM   Of course I do.

He sits down facing her and they hold hands like they do in couples' counselling. They take the moment to breathe together before starting again.

LISET   Why didn't you tell me what happened to your hand?

JIM   I did. I told you I broke it at work.

LISET   Yes, but you didn't tell me you broke it by punching the side of your truck.

JIM   Who told you that?

LISET   Barb did.

JIM   Yeah, well, maybe Barb shouldn't be putting her nose where it doesn't belong.

LISET   Dale told her, and then she told me because they're worried about you.

JIM   I wish people would mind their own business.

LISET   She thinks you were having a panic attack. Is that true?

JIM   She doesn't know what she's talking about.

LISET   She's a nurse.

JIM   It wasn't a panic attack.

LISET   Dale told Barb that you had to pull the truck over because you couldn't catch your breath. That you stepped outside and then you got really upset and punched the side of the truck.

JIM   So?

LISET   So, you broke your hand. That's not good.

JIM   It was a stupid mistake.

LISET   How long have you been having panic attacks?

JIM   They're not panic attacks.

LISET   If something like that is happening to you, I don't want to
         hear it from Barb. I want to hear it from you.

JIM   And what am I supposed to say? "Hey, babe, I keep having
         these moments where I can't breathe and it feels like some-
         one is standing on my chest and I can't calm down and I
         don't know how to stop it once it starts!"

LISET   Yes, that is exactly what I want you to say!

JIM   Ah, come on!

LISET   No, I'm serious.

JIM   So am I.

LISET   This is about Craig, isn't it?

JIM   Oh, don't start with that, I'm not in the mood.

LISET   You never talk about him.

JIM   Yes I do.

LISET   When?

JIM   I don't know; I don't keep track.

LISET I do and it never happens. Like NEVER. And neither does Paul.

JIM   Paul? What does he have to do with this?

LISET Everything. How's he doing?

JIM   I don't know; I haven't seen him.

LISET Exactly.

JIM   What.

LISET You're totally avoiding him.

JIM   No I'm not.

LISET Yes you are. Lucille says he's not doing very well.

JIM   What am I supposed to do about that?

LISET He's your best friend.

JIM   So?

LISET So, I think it would be good if you went over there to see how he's doing.

JIM   No, we don't do that.

LISET Do what?

JIM   That. The touchy-feely stuff.

LISET	Oh, Jim, grow up.
JIM	You wouldn't understand.
LISET	Then find another reason to be there.
JIM	Like what?
LISET	Like, I don't know . . . Bring him back his Shop-Vac. It's been sitting on the front porch for over a year.
JIM	That's dumb.
LISET	No, it's a reason to drop by. Then the two of you can hang out, have a couple of beers, smoke a few cigarettes, and then, when things feel right, you can ask him how he's doing. Easy peasy.
JIM	I'm not doing that.
LISET	Why not?
JIM	'Cause I don't want to.
LISET	Jim—
JIM	No, I don't want to talk about this anymore.
LISET	Oh really?
JIM	Yes, really.
LISET	That's too bad 'cause I'm not done yet.
JIM	Ah, would you stop it, woman!

LISET   Don't talk to me like that.

JIM   Then don't push me like that.

LISET   You keep this up and you'll be sleeping on the couch for a very long time.

JIM   Not in my house I won't.

LISET   You mean our house.

JIM   No, I mean my house. I pay the bills here—I sleep where I want.

LISET   Oh, you want to bet?

JIM   Yes, yes I do.

She takes one step towards him and he flinches. They are at a stalemate. She slowly walks past him and out of the room.

SCENE 9—FOX STORY PART 3

JIM   The fox didn't know what else to do, so he asked Mother
        Earth to help him find his story. But she remained silent
        as she always had, and the fox watched the sun rest on
        the edge of the horizon. His story would end in all the
        colours of the evening sky and there was nothing he could
        do about it. You see, since there was no story to continue,
        there was no story to tell, so the fox jumped off the edge
        of the earth with the beautiful sun and was never seen
        again.

SCENE 10—ONE-YEAR ANNIVERSARY

PAUL *enters dressed in warm gear carrying a flashlight. He has a small map with him.*

PAUL   See anything?

JIM   *(off)* No.

JIM enters. PAUL is looking at the map.

            Maybe she went back to the house.

PAUL   Maybe.

JIM   Should we head back?

PAUL   I don't know. We still have to check over by the Trans-Canada.

JIM   You really think she'd go that far?

PAUL   I don't know . . .

PAUL *reaches into his pocket, grabs two flares, and hands one to JIM.*

How's about this. You go back taking Camp Road 25 in case she went that way. I'll head over to the Trans-Canada. If one of us finds her we set off a flare. Sound good?

JIM   Yeah. You gonna be all right?

PAUL   Not until we find her.

JIM exits.

SCENE 11—TEN MONTHS AFTER DEATH

LUCILLE sits alone in the dark. A long time passes before PAUL walks into the house. He doesn't see her.

LUCILLE   What time is it?

PAUL   Oh hey. What are you doing sitting in the dark?

LUCILLE   Nothing.

PAUL   You're just sitting there by yourself?

LUCILLE   Yes, I'm just sitting here by myself.

PAUL   It's almost eleven o'clock.

LUCILLE   I know.

PAUL   You okay?

He goes over to kiss her on the cheek and she pulls away.

             What?

LUCILLE   You've been drinking.

PAUL   Sorry, I stopped in at Hap's for a few beers after work.

LUCILLE   How many is a few?

PAUL   Why does it matter?

LUCILLE   It doesn't, I guess.

   Beat.

PAUL   Fine. I went to the bar, we had some beers. I didn't keep
           track 'cause I didn't think I had to. I drank I don't know,
           six or eight beers, but they were bottles. I threw some darts
           with Dale, went to the washroom once, smoked a cigarette
           on the way home, and parked the truck in my usual spot.
           Are we done with the third degree?

LUCILLE   You don't have to be defensive about it.

PAUL   It kinda feels like I do.

LUCILLE   That's too bad.

PAUL   My thoughts exactly.

LUCILLE   Why do you drive home like that?

PAUL   I was fine.

LUCILLE   Try telling that to the police when they pull you over.

PAUL   Loo—

LUCILLE   No, you never used to stay out like this.

PAUL   I lost track of time.

LUCILLE   You didn't even call to tell me where you were.

PAUL   I didn't think I had to.

LUCILLE   You don't have to. But it would have been nice if you had.

PAUL   Right . . . I need a beer.

He walks off into the kitchen.

LUCILLE   You work tomorrow.

PAUL   *(off)* So what? WHOA! What happened in here!?!

LUCILLE   Don't worry, I'll clean it up.

He comes out of the kitchen.

PAUL   There is glass everywhere.

LUCILLE   It's my mother's china.

PAUL   All of it?

LUCILLE   Yes, all of it.

PAUL   That's a lot of china.

LUCILLE   I know.

PAUL   But why is it broken all over the kitchen floor?

LUCILLE   Because that's where I broke it.

PAUL   You did it on purpose?

LUCILLE   Yes. It felt good. We should break more stuff.

PAUL   Why would you do something like that?

LUCILLE   Because it doesn't mean anything to me anymore.

PAUL   What are you talking about?

LUCILLE   I was saving them for Craig when he got married.

PAUL   Oh, Loo.

LUCILLE   What do we do with all this stuff? My parents' wedding rings, your dad's tools. And what about our family photos? They don't mean anything to anyone else.

PAUL   They mean something to us.

LUCILLE   We should have a huge bonfire.

PAUL   No we shouldn't.

LUCILLE   We could get rid of everything.

PAUL   Stop talking like that. You're not making any sense.

   PAUL *turns to go back into the kitchen.*

LUCILLE   So that's it? The conversation is over?

PAUL   What do you want me to say?

LUCILLE   Something, anything would be helpful.

PAUL   I can't talk to you when you're like this. We'll speak in the
            morning.

LUCILLE   No, I'm not waiting for you to sleep it off so we can have
            a conversation.

PAUL   What are you talking about?

LUCILLE   I can smell you from here.

PAUL   Why do you always have to be so dramatic? Breaking all
            the china! Was that really the answer you were looking for?

LUCILLE   At the time, yes!

PAUL   I don't even know what to say to that.

LUCILLE   Forget it, I'll clean it up.

PAUL   That's not the point. You do this all the time—you create
            drama. It's hard enough to deal with everything else going
            on here, now I have to deal with this? I mean, come on!

LUCILLE   Oh, I'm sorry, I didn't mean to inconvenience you with my
            feelings.

PAUL   You sound like Craig when you talk like that.

LUCILLE   There it is. Even now you can't help yourself.

PAUL   Here we go again with the dramatics.

LUCILLE   Nothing he ever did was good enough for you. You always
            had to make a comment about something.

PAUL   That's not true.

LUCILLE   You never let up no matter what. Just like your father did with you.

PAUL   Hey, my old man did the best he could in the situation.

LUCILLE   He was a bully.

PAUL   Well if you mean he didn't coddle me, you're right, he didn't. You, on the other hand, you wouldn't let the boy be. You were always trying to protect him from everything.

LUCILLE   I'm his mother.

PAUL   You never let him stand on his own two feet.

LUCILLE   He was suffering from depression. You never took the time to understand what that means.

PAUL   Don't give me that. I supported him. When he was struggling I got him into hockey; I signed him up for baseball. I went to every one of his games.

LUCILLE   You gave him a hard time about taking medication.

PAUL   Why is it always about medication?

LUCILLE   Because he needed it!

PAUL   No, he needed his family, and instead he pushed us away.

LUCILLE   It's a disease, Paul.

PAUL	Don't give me that. If I had spoken to my father that way, he would have beat me into the middle of next week.
LUCILLE	Yes, well, that says a lot about his parenting skills.
PAUL	Well he must have done something right because I'm still here.
LUCILLE	You see? That's exactly what I'm talking about. After all that's happened you're still hard on him.
PAUL	No. He gave up, and I can't forgive him for that.
LUCILLE	That's a healthy way of looking at it.
PAUL	Well it's a lot better than sitting at home in the dark feeling sorry for myself.
LUCILLE	Or maybe I should start drinking my face off every night and pretending like nothing's happened.
PAUL	Or maybe I'll go break all the china in the kitchen and maybe I'll feel better!
LUCILLE	I was upset!
PAUL	No, you were unstable! And you wonder where Craig got it from!

She slaps him. Silence.

We'll talk in the morning.

He turns to walk out.

LUCILLE   I'm leaving.

PAUL   Fine.

LUCILLE   —I'll stay with my sister. You can have the house. I don't want it.

PAUL   The house? What are you talking about?

LUCILLE   I can't do this anymore—

PAUL   —Okay, stop right there. You're being over-dramatic.

LUCILLE   You can't say those things to me and then take it back.

She starts to gather her stuff.

PAUL   I didn't mean it like that.

LUCILLE   Yes you did.

PAUL tries to hold her.

PAUL   Don't leave.

LUCILLE   Let me go.

PAUL   Listen, I was upset. I take it back.

LUCILLE   Let go of me.

PAUL   Loo, please—

LUCILLE   NOW!

He lets her go.

PAUL   I didn't mean it.

LUCILLE   Yes you did. You're angry with Craig but mostly you're angry with me. You blame me for what happened and I can't do this anymore.

Beat.

PAUL   Fine then. Go. And while you're at it go hang yourself and then everyone can blame me for that too!

She is at a loss. She grabs what she can and walks out.

SCENE 12—DAY BEFORE THE ANNIVERSARY

It is late in the evening. LUCILLE *is outside wrapped in a blanket holding the egg.* LISET *comes outside.*

LISET   Hey. What are you still doing out here? It's almost midnight.

LUCILLE   I was enjoying the company.

LISET *clocks the fox. She reacts negatively.*

LISET   It's getting pretty late. Why don't you come inside?

LUCILLE   I'm good. Don't feel like you have to wait up for me.

LISET *looks out at the fox.*

LISET   Hey, give us some privacy, we're talking here.

LUCILLE   Please don't yell at him like that, you'll scare him away.

LISET   Trust me, it doesn't work. I yell at him all the time.

LUCILLE   That's not funny.

LISET   I'm not trying to be funny. Besides, I don't trust wild animals near the house.

LUCILLE   Just leave us alone, please?

LISET   Um . . . You know it doesn't need you taking care of it, right? In fact, it's probably better if you left it alone. Then, maybe it wouldn't hang around the house so much.

LUCILLE   I don't do anything to make him stay. He does that on his own.

LISET   Uh huh.

LUCILLE   Besides, I like that he hangs out here.

LISET   You would.

LUCILLE   Yeah, I would . . . It feels like he's protecting us.

LISET gives her a look.

       What?

LISET   Nothing.

Silence. Both women are looking out at the fox.

       He is beautiful, I'll give him that.

LUCILLE   He is, isn't he?

LISET   Yeah. He's pretty cute.

LUCILLE   Have you ever seen a fox behave like that before?

LISET   No.

LUCILLE   Me neither.

LISET   He's an odd one, that's for sure.

   Beat.

LUCILLE   Can I ask you something?

LISET   Sure.

LUCILLE   I'm being serious.

LISET   So am I.

LUCILLE   No, like serious, serious.

LISET   Like so serious you had to say it twice?

LUCILLE   You know what, forget it.

LISET   Hey, you don't want to talk about it, then we won't talk about it.

LUCILLE   Good.

LISET   Good.

   Beat.

LUCILLE   But I do want to talk about it.

LISET   I know you do, so spit it out.

LUCILLE   Fine, but promise me you'll keep an open mind.

LISET   Sure.

LUCILLE   Promise.

LISET   I promise.

    LUCILLE gives her a look.

             What else do you want from me?

LUCILLE   Nothing . . . I'm not sure how to say this . . . Does the fox
             remind you of someone?

LISET   Um, no. Why? Does he remind you of someone?

LUCILLE   Maybe.

LISET   Maybe?

LUCILLE   Like what if the fox is . . .

LISET   What.

LUCILLE   I don't know . . . what if he's . . . you know.

LISET   No I don't.

LUCILLE   What if he's Craig, who's come back to tell me he's okay.

LISET   You're kidding me, right?

    Beat.

             Oh, Loo.

LUCILLE   Forget I said anything.

LISET   No, you caught me off guard, give me a sec.

LUCILLE   You think I'm crazy.

LISET   No, I think you're grieving.

LUCILLE   That's a nice way of saying crazy.

LISET   You know what? Maybe you're right, maybe I'm not the best person to be talking to you about this.

LUCILLE   But you're my sister.

LISET   Yeah, but I'm also a Catholic.

LUCILLE   So?

LISET   So I don't believe people come back as furry little creatures to visit their loved ones. I just don't.

LUCILLE   Well you don't have to be rude about it.

LISET   I'm not being rude; I'm being honest.

LUCILLE   Oh, is that what that is?

LISET   Listen, I know you're feeling a bit crazy right now and I get that. I'm trying to support you here—

LUCILLE   I'm not crazy. Why would you say that?

LISET   You think the fox is Craig coming back to visit you. Think about what that sounds like for a second.

LUCILLE   This was a big mistake.

LISET   I am trying to give you some perspective here. You have
            to start dealing with the fact that life goes on.

LUCILLE   My life ended the day Craig died.

LISET   I know it might feel that way but you're still here, and you
            can't just sit in my backyard all day pretending that life
            isn't going on all around you.

LUCILLE   Is that what you think I'm doing?

LISET   Not all the time. But a lot. Yes.

    There is a beat and then LUCILLE *starts to laugh.*

            What?

LUCILLE   Thank you.

LISET   For what?

LUCILLE   For giving me perspective. I'll be gone by the end of
            the week.

LISET   Gone? But why?

LUCILLE   I need to get my own place.

LISET   No you don't.

LUCILLE   Yes I do. Everyone keeps telling me how I should be griev-
            ing and I'm done with it.

LISET   That is not what I was doing.

LUCILLE   That's exactly what you were doing. No one gets to tell me
            how I feel about anything anymore. I'll be gone by the end
            of the week.

    LUCILLE turns and walks away.

LISET   Loo, don't leave, please? LOO!

SCENE 13—TWO MONTHS AFTER DEATH

JIM and LISET's home. There is a knock at the door. JIM opens it to find PAUL standing there.

JIM   Hey, man.

PAUL   Hey.

JIM   You wanna come in?

PAUL   No, I just need a sec.

JIM   Sure . . . You wanna beer?

PAUL   No, I promised Loo I'd be back soon.

JIM   Okay.

PAUL   I gotta say this . . . Why you and not me?

JIM   I'm sorry?

PAUL   Why didn't he call me?

JIM   Oh geez, Paul, I don't know.

PAUL   I'm his dad. I'm the one he should have called.

JIM   Like I said—

PAUL   Was he upset with me?

JIM   I don't think so.

PAUL   Did he mention anything?

JIM   No, he just . . . called, and asked me to go fishing.

PAUL   That's it?

JIM   Yeah, that's it.

PAUL   You wouldn't lie to me, would you?

JIM   No. Why would I do that?

PAUL   I don't know, maybe he said something you didn't want to
           tell me.

JIM   Hey, man, nothing like that happened.

PAUL   You promise?

JIM   I promise.

    Beat.

PAUL   How's the Chevy?

JIM   What does that have to do with anything?

PAUL   Dale mentioned the clutch is sticking again.

JIM   Yeah, it was, but it's fine now.

PAUL   Well if the clutch is sticking it might be part of a bigger problem—

JIM   It's not.

PAUL   How would you know?

JIM   Because, I fixed it.

PAUL   You fixed it?

JIM   Yeah, it was easy.

PAUL   No it's not.

JIM   Well, it's not that hard.

PAUL   Says the guy who can't even fix a friggin' toaster.

JIM   I can fix a friggin' toaster, thank you very much.

PAUL   Oh yeah, then how'd you fix it?

JIM   I did the . . . anyways it works fine now.

PAUL   Really? Did you replace the clutch pin, because the pin needs to be reattached to the engine valve in order for the carburetor to work.

JIM   Yeah, something like that.

PAUL   Why are you lying to me?

JIM   Mmmmm, I'm not.

PAUL   There is no such thing as a clutch pin.

JIM   Well, I did something that worked.

PAUL   How'd you fix it?

JIM   Is it really that hard for you to believe that I fixed something?

PAUL   Yes, yes it is.

JIM   Nice friend you are.

PAUL   Look, I have fixed your vehicles for over twenty years now and there's a reason for it.

JIM   —Paul—

PAUL   No, look at me. If you're going to lie I want you to look me in the eyes when you do it . . . How'd you fix the clutch?

JIM   . . . I . . . I didn't . . . I took it to Edward's.

PAUL   . . . You took it to Edward's Garage?

JIM   Yeah.

PAUL   You've been my best friend my whole life and you took it to him?

JIM   He was at the bar one night and we got to talking. He told me to bring it in so I did.

PAUL   You always bring it to me.

JIM   It was a one-time thing.

PAUL   What aren't you telling me?

JIM   Nothing!

   PAUL *gets up in* JIM's *face.*

PAUL   You're lying. You can't even look me in the eyes.

JIM   Hey, back off, man.

PAUL   Or what?

JIM   I'm serious. Take a step back.

PAUL   Maybe I don't want to.

   PAUL *pushes* JIM.

JIM   Don't. I'm serious.

PAUL   You think you're better than me?

JIM   You need to calm down.

PAUL   What if I don't want to calm down.

   PAUL *pushes him again and they grab at each other.* JIM *gets*
   PAUL *in a headlock and gets him to the ground.* PAUL *is pinned.*
   They wrestle awkwardly.

   Let me go!

JIM   Not until you settle down!

PAUL continues to try and get at JIM but he has PAUL securely pinned. JIM holds PAUL until he gives up. JIM stands up. Silence. JIM offers PAUL his hand.

               . Here. Don't be stubborn.

PAUL   I don't need your pity.

JIM   It's not pity.

PAUL gets up.

PAUL   I thought you were my friend.

JIM   I am.

PAUL   No, you're a liar.

PAUL turns and walks away.

SCENE 14—ONE-YEAR ANNIVERSARY

The deck. LISET *steps outside after dinner to gain her composure. She needs a moment, but before that happens she sees the fox and is immediately upset.*

LISET   Ah come on! Would you just leave us alone, for God's sakes? You're not helping, *this* is not helping. It's not helping her and it's definitely not helping me . . . Oh you are a piece of work, I tell ya. Go on, get out of here. I SAID GET OUT OF HERE! Oh you are so lucky I can't get my hands on you right now. If I could I would grab you and I would shakeshakeshakeshakeshake until there was nothing left of you! AND JUST BECAUSE I'M YELLING AT YOU DOESN'T MEAN I THINK YOU ARE WHO SHE SAYS YOU ARE, 'CAUSE YOU'RE NOT! Yeah yeah yeah, tilt your head, you smug little . . . What do you want from me? Tell me, I'll do it—I will. 'Cause there's nothing left. You've taken it all away, and now it feels like . . . like I loved you too much, 'cause it hurts all the time—my chest literally hurts when I breathe, because I miss you so much, and it doesn't go away, and it never will, and I know it won't, and I can't do anything about it, and it makes me so mad. I am so mad at you and I have never been mad at you in my whole life ever. And I can't, I can't do this anymore . . . WELL, DON'T JUST STAND THERE. SAY SOMETHING, WOULD YOU? . . . Yeah, I didn't think so . . . You're nothing but a fox . . . a stupid little fox, and I don't want you hanging around here anymore.

LISET leaves and JIM enters looking for her.

JIM   Liz?

LISET returns with a gun.

LISET   Out of my way.

JIM   Whoa, whoa, whoa. Hon, look at me. You don't want to do this. Put the gun down.

LISET   No, I'm sorry, I have to do this.

JIM   No you don't. Listen to me. Put the gun down.

JIM slowly walks up to her.

LISET   I can't have him around here anymore. I'm sorry.

In one swift movement JIM tilts the gun up and it goes off in the air. The fox runs off.

THAT'S RIGHT, RUN AWAY!

She grabs the egg.

And take this with you!

JIM   NO, LIZ!

She goes to throw it but JIM stops her, accidentally breaking the egg in her hand as LUCILLE walks in.

LISET   Oh no.

LUCILLE What's wrong?

JIM Nothing, everything is fine.

LUCILLE What happened?

JIM It's the egg. There was an accident.

LUCILLE What do you mean?

LISET It was me. I broke it.

LUCILLE Why the gunshot?

JIM Oh. Well, um—

LUCILLE Jim, why do you have the gun?

LISET I was trying to scare him away.

LUCILLE You didn't!

JIM No, nothing happened. The gun went off in the air.

LUCILLE turns to leave.

LISET Where are you going?

LUCILLE I need to make sure he's okay.

LISET We'll come with you.

LUCILLE No you won't. You've done enough already.

LUCILLE turns and runs off. Silence.

JIM   Babe.

LISET   I've really done it this time, haven't I?

JIM   No . . . Well maybe a bit. It'll be fine, it will. She just needs some time to cool off.

LISET   Maybe we should follow her to make sure she's all right?

JIM   No, we should give her some space.

LISET   I didn't mean it.

JIM   I know you didn't. Come here.

They hug.

It'll be okay.

They exit.

SCENE 15—ONE DAY BEFORE ANNIVERSARY

PAUL   Hello. Most of you know me, but for those of you that
don't my name is Paul. I've been coming to this family
support group for almost a year now. I usually don't say
much at these things. I'm not good at this stuff, but tomorrow marks the one-year anniversary of my son's death, so
I thought it might be good to say something . . . I have a
hard time talking about him . . . His name was Craig . . .
He was a sweet kid. Gentle. Really gentle. Like I could
never get him to lay a bodycheck in hockey because he
just didn't want to hurt anybody . . . And that was him
in a nutshell . . . I never know what to say when people
ask me why he did it . . . Nothing fits . . . So my buddy
Riel, he used to work for the ministry fighting forest fires.
The year before he retired the government introduced
this program where university students were brought in
to help out. Riel was one of the senior guys so he was put
in charge of one of the crews. Now, these kids had only
been on the job for a couple of weeks. Enough time for
some basic training, but that's about it. None of them had
any real experience working on a forest fire. But it was
a really dry summer that year and within days Riel and
his crew find themselves helping out on the front lines.
They were called in to set up what's called "a fire line."
They spent the morning digging it up. By midday they had
worked themselves into a small valley. Thing is, they didn't
know the wind had changed direction, and it picked up

pretty quick, and before they knew it the fire was on top of them. Riel knew they were in trouble. He also knew they couldn't outrun the fire, so he told the crew that they would have to turn and walk directly through the flames if they wanted to survive. Some of the kids refused. They were scared; they thought it was better idea to try and run away from it. Riel pleaded with them, begged them to follow his instructions and trust his experience. But they wouldn't listen. And before he knew it they were running away. He didn't have time to chase after them so he had to save the ones he could. He turned and walked them right into the fire . . . And he was right. The sixteen kids that followed him that day survived. The four who didn't died . . . because no one can outrun a forest fire . . . Now you're probably wondering what this has to do with my son . . . I didn't know what was going on with Craig at the time. We didn't talk like that. Him and his mom did but I . . . I don't know, it was always harder for us . . . and I wasn't there for him when he needed me. I wasn't there to walk him through the fire. Instead, he tried to outrun it, except no one can outrun depression. But, boy, he did his best. And that's all I could have asked of him. Thank you.

SCENE 16—ONE-YEAR ANNIVERSARY

The garage. PAUL *is in his workshop.*

JIM   Paul? You there?

JIM enters.

PAUL   Huh . . . Sorry, we're closed.

JIM   Paul, please—

PAUL   Edward's is open late, maybe he can help you out.

JIM   Just . . . give me a second, would you. I need your help.

PAUL   Sorry, I only help my friends.

JIM   Really?

PAUL   Really.

JIM turns away to walk off. Then stops himself.

JIM   No. No, you don't get to be angry at me about this. It's not my fault he didn't call you. You want to know what happened? Fine. He called me that morning like he always did on the weekends. He said, "Hey, Uncle Jim, you want go fishing?" I said, "I don't know, kiddo, it's a bit cold out there, eh? First frost is down." "Please? I need to get out of the house." I thought about it for a sec, and then I said, "Why not. I'll meet you down at Aaron's Point in an hour." "Thanks, Uncle Jim." "No worries, kiddo. And don't forget to bring your long johns 'cause you can't borrow mine." He laughed . . . Huh . . . I hung up the phone, got my stuff together. I stopped at Timmie's, grabbed a coffee for me and a hot chocolate for him, like I always did, then I headed out. When I pulled up his car was already there. I thought, wow, the kid got here before I did, that's a first. So I grabbed my stuff and I headed up to where we usually meet . . . I didn't see him anywhere so I walked down to the river. Nothing . . . I called out his name. Nothing. Then I turned around . . . Somehow he'd managed to get a belt around one of the tree branches . . . he was . . . I grabbed onto him, tried holding him up, but it was too late . . . I knew I had to cut him down, so I did . . . He was cold, like cold cold, so I took off my coat and I wrapped him up in it . . . we just sat there, me holding him tight listening to the river . . . I don't know how long it was before I pulled out my phone and called Kev at the police station. I told him what happened so he drove out. Annie followed him with the ambulance, no sirens, no lights . . . He came over, sat down beside me . . . He said, "Jim, take all the time you need. You let us know when you're ready to let him go. But I promise you we're gonna take good care of him." He promised, so I did. I let him go . . . You want to know why he didn't call you? He didn't want you to be the one who found him. He was trying to protect you. At least that's what my counsellor tells me.

PAUL   Then why call you?

JIM   I don't know. We're still working that one out.

Beat.

PAUL   What do you need help with?

JIM   Oh, yeah, it's Lucille. She ran off into the woods and hasn't
        come back.

PAUL   Why would she do that?

JIM   Well she's been watching this little fox. It's been hanging
        around the house lately. Liz and her got into a fight. Liz
        tried to shoot the fox and then she broke the egg.

PAUL   The egg?

JIM   Yeah apparently the fox gave her the egg, so she took it as
        a sign the fox was Craig.

PAUL   I'm sorry, what?

JIM   Yeah, uh, she thinks the fox in our backyard is Craig.

PAUL   *(sighs)* Of course she does.

JIM   But now she's run off looking for him.

PAUL   In the woods.

JIM   And it's getting late and we're starting to worry about her.

PAUL   Are you sure she's not just over at Barb's or something?

JIM   No, Liset's been on the phone all evening. No one's seen
        her . . .

PAUL   Well she doesn't want me finding her.

JIM   You know the backwoods better than anyone else. I figured if we both went out there looking it wouldn't be long before one of us found her.

Beat.

PAUL   Fine, I'll do it.

JIM   Great.

PAUL   On one condition: if she gets angry 'cause I'm out there— that's on you.

JIM   Fair enough.

PAUL   Is Liz okay with this?

JIM   Oh yeah, she's the one who suggested it.

PAUL   Good to see you're still bad at lying. Let me get my coat.

PAUL goes to leave but stops.

        Hey, I uh . . . I appreciate what you said about—

JIM   Just grab your coat.

PAUL   Right.

Both men exit.

SCENE 17—FOX STORY PART 4

LUCILLE   And when the sun returned the next morning, life continued as it always had, and stories continued as they always do. For you see, the fox did not understand that our stories are not just ours to tell. Other people tell them too, because our stories live in the people around us. And when we lose our way, when we feel like we can't remember our own story anymore, and that it might be coming to an end—that everything is going to be okay: because when we can't tell our own story, the people in our lives tell our story for us. Even when it remains hidden from our ears, when we think it has gone away and will not come back again, I assure you, it will. For you see, that is the true magic of stories: your story lives in me and my story lives in you. So, little fox, remember this—your story remains safe, in the most secret of all secret places, in the utmost cherished and delicate parts of the heart of the ones you love, I promise you that. And when you need it, when the light is dim and the path is long, it will be there for you to guide you home. I guarantee it: because you are loved.

SCENE 18—ONE-YEAR ANNIVERSARY

Night. We hear the wind through the canopy of trees mixed with intermittent sounds of the forest. We see LUCILLE *sitting by herself. Close by her the fox lies motionless.* PAUL *enters but keeps his distance. After a time she speaks.*

LUCILLE   You don't have to hide back there.

PAUL   Sorry . . . I wasn't sure if you wanted to see me.

LUCILLE   Hello.

PAUL   Hi.

LUCILLE   He hasn't moved since I got here.

PAUL *walks over and checks. The fox has indeed passed away.*

PAUL   Sorry, Loo. Looks like he might have been hit by a car . . . The Trans-Canada is just . . . Anyways. He's gone.

LUCILLE   I didn't want to leave him out here on his own.

PAUL   Of course not.

LUCILLE   He looks so peaceful lying there, part of me was hoping he'd jump up and run away.

Beat.

PAUL   Would you like me to leave?

LUCILLE   Would you go if I said yes?

PAUL   Probably not.

LUCILLE   Then by all means.

PAUL   People are worried about you, Loo.

LUCILLE   I know.

PAUL   Will you let me take you home?

LUCILLE   I wish he had left us a note.

PAUL   Me too.

LUCILLE   He had a lunch packed and his little chess set with him. Why would he bring those things if he was going to . . .

PAUL   I don't know.

LUCILLE   I should have seen it coming.

PAUL   No one did.

LUCILLE   But I'm his mother. I should have seen it.

PAUL   He was good at hiding it from us.

LUCILLE   I didn't kiss him when I left for work that morning. I was in a hurry and I forgot.

PAUL   We were both in a rush—

LUCILLE   Sometimes I wonder if I had said goodbye to him—

PAUL   You can't think like that.

LUCILLE   But I do . . . I have this old message he left on my phone.
            I play it over and over again 'cause I'm afraid I'll forget
            what his voice sounds like.

PAUL   I keep thinking he's going to walk into the shop like he
            used to. Sometimes I hear him calling for me, or worse I
            go to ask him to do something and I have to remind myself
            he's gone. It's like my heart doesn't speak to my head any-
            more . . . Temperature is starting to drop.

LUCILLE   I'm not leaving him out here on his own.

PAUL   What would you like to do?

LUCILLE   I don't know. Actually, there is one thing.

PAUL   What?

LUCILLE   Would you sit with me for a bit?

PAUL   Of course . . . If you're cold I could build us a fire—

LUCILLE   No, I'm good.

    Beat.

PAUL   If you want I can carry him back to the house tonight. We
            can give him a proper burial in the morning.

LUCILLE   Maybe.

Beat.

PAUL   Or we could bring him back here in the morning. Do it
            somewhere around here.

LUCILLE   I don't want to think about it right now.

PAUL   Right . . . What if I was to make us one of those—

LUCILLE   There is no way to fix this, so please stop trying.

PAUL   Sorry.

LUCILLE   Don't be. I know what you're trying to do; I appreciate it,
            I do, but please just sit with me.

PAUL   Sure.

He does. A long silence. We feel them breathe.

            It's never going to get better, is it?

LUCILLE   No. But it will get easier . . . Do you remember the book
            we used to read to him before bed?

PAUL   *Le Petit Renard.*

LUCILLE   *The Little Fox.*

PAUL   Wore the damn thing out. I had to put duct tape down the
            spine just to keep it together.

LUCILLE   He was our little fox, wasn't he?

PAUL   Yes, yes he was. And now he's gone.

LUCILLE   No, he's here; I can feel him.

PAUL   I can't. I wish I could, but I can't.

LUCILLE   Well you'll have to trust me when I say that he is.

Beat.

Once there was a fox.

She looks at him expectantly.

PAUL   What are you doing?

LUCILLE   Once there was a fox.

PAUL   Loo, please.

He sighs.

(reluctantly) Who lived in the forest.

LUCILLE   You do remember.

PAUL   Of course I do. Read the damn thing at least a thousand times.

LUCILLE   And he had a magical gift for storytelling.

PAUL   Can we not do this, please?

LUCILLE   He was so good at telling stories that animals would come from all around and from far away just to hear them being told.

PAUL   . . . And the fox would spend all of his days making up story after story and telling them to anyone who would listen.

LUCILLE   But one day, as sometimes happen, things changed.

They lean into each other. The lights fade as the couple is silhouetted. We hear the following phone message as the lights fade to black. It is a slice of life, a casual, everyday message that anyone would leave his or her mother on a typical day.

CRAIG   *(voice-over)* "Hey, Mom, I'm just heading off to work now. Sorry, I lost track of time so I had to leave my dishes, but I'll wash them when I get home, I promise. Anyhoo, Mike and I are going to try and catch a movie after work, so don't worry about me for dinner. Oh, and Dad wants tacos tonight so I took some ground beef out of the freezer—and yes, I put it on a plate. I'll see you tonight after the show. I love you. Bu-bye."

The end.

ACKNOWLEDGEMENTS

First and foremost my sincere gratitude to all the artists who contributed their time and talent to making this play what it is today. It truly does take a village to raise an artist and I am grateful to have so many kind and generous people in my life. In no particular order, I would like to give my thanks to the village.

To my beautiful wife Catherine, how lucky am I to share my life with you. You continue to fascinate and inspire me. To my mom, whose love and compassion has no bounds; all the kindness that I have in me comes from her. To my sisters Bryce, Shannon, and Penny, who helped shape the person I am today. To their husbands, Todd and Chrisso, and to the kids Taylor, Garrett, Issac, and River—big love to all of you. To my in-laws Ginette, David, Elisabeth: *merci pour votre générosité et votre soutien.* To my Turpin and Barker family, who always make me laugh and have taught me the value of good storytelling. To my friends, who support and love me, give me a couch to sleep on when I travel, let me hang out with their kids, take me out for beer and nachos, come to see my shows, play on my hockey team, and pick me up when I fall down. Your love and support is paramount to me. To my business partner Wade Vroom, who shouldered all of the responsibilities in our little mini-donut business so I could chase my artistic endeavours. I am forever thankful for your friendship. To Genne for her grace, her wisdom, her love and friendship, and to Anna for taking such good care of the mutual furry love of our lives, Hoito. To Joshua, Justin, Jerry, and Carol, the Speers and Merkleys who welcomed me into their family and remain in my heart always. To Carol—I think about you often and I am grateful for the time we had together and for all that you did for me.

To the Koop family, who showed me what grace and love can do in the face of tragedy. To my auntie Jane and uncle Tuomo for teaching me the true value of life and of love in all of its difficult, complicated, and beautiful forms. To Daniel, Craig, and Aaron: all three had kind eyes and warm smiles. I have tried to honour your memories in this writing.

To my co-conspirator Eli Ham, who did all the heavy lifting, literally and metaphorically, and who was my moral support throughout the evolution of this play. It would not have seen the stage without his commitment, love, and sacrifice. To my other co-conspirator Donna-Michelle St. Bernard, whose impact on my work is immense; her support for me as a playwright is invaluable. She inspires me with her work, her friendship, her love and generosity.

To Leah-Simone Bowen for her friendship and support throughout this process. Our conversations keep me going, make me laugh to tears, and allow me to do this work with an open heart.

To Imago Theatre and particularly Micheline Chevrier, who helped me polish the play before it premiered at the SummerWorks Festival, whose friendship and mentorship have guided me in all the best ways possible, and whose strength and vision are an inspiration. To Emma Tibaldo and Playwrights' Workshop Montréal, whose collaboration with artists has an immense impact on their work, and whose support is a blessing. To Eileen Smith at the SpringWorks Festival—I am humbled by her support of my work since the beginning of my playwriting career. To David Storch, whose initial thoughts on the play helped shape what it is today. I aspire to be the artist he is. To Tara Beagan, who supported me at a time when I doubted I could finish the play, and who was part of the selection committee for SummerWorks, along with Guillermo Verdecchia. To Brian Quirt and Jenna Rodgers at the Banff Playwrights Lab for working the schedule so I could have time with actors to hear my words. To Antoni Cimolino and the Stratford Festival's Playwrights Retreat for giving me time to write and see shows, and be with some of the best playwrights in the business. Thank you to Keira Loughran for her support and guidance, and to Bob White for giving me the biggest note to make the play better, and for his candour. To the Blyth Festival for giving me a day with actors so I could hear the play. To Gil Garratt for giving me the second biggest note that shifted the play to what it is now. To Playwrights Canada Press, Annie, Blake and the staff who have graciously supported me and who come out to see my work. I am honoured to be part of the PLCN family. To Native Earth Performing Arts, who gave me my first home as a playwright, and my first home as an artistic director.

The production of this play would not have been possible without the support of the Toronto Arts Council and the Ontario Arts Council. To all of my friends and colleagues at the Canada Council for the Arts. My time at Council was invaluable. You are all missed. I carry you in my heart.

To the donors of the SummerWorks production: Deb Erb, Travis Murphy, Ann Rose, Anne Koizumi, Bryce Voca, Christine Rambukkana, Erin Tomlinson, Ginette Frenette-Butler, David and Elisabeth Butler, Irene Barker, Issac and River Powell, Kate and Patrick Gauthier, Kate and Ali Taylor, Keli and Sal Cristofaro, Marc Bondy, Michael Soulard, my mom Michelle Turpin, my cousin Michelle Turpin, Marcus Lundgren, Wendy Greenwood, Nadene Schuster, Mike Ledermueller, Rod Keith, Khris and Brad Adams, Peter Gardiner-Harding, Pierre Lake, Rena Polley and Jim Cuddy, Robert and Jen Kingston, Shauna Wilton, Steven Burley and Jacquelyn Pijper, Val Hendrickson, Victor Dolhal, Yvette Nolan and Philip Adams, Ronnie Kaplansky and Liz White, Warren Ham, Martin Gero, and Brendan Gall.

To the workshop actors who made this all possible—Marcus Lundgren, Rachel Jones, Jeff Irving, Karen Parker, David Mackett, Jamie Lee Shebelski, Anita La Selva, Sarah Evans, Skye Brandon, Christopher Hunt, Jenna-Lee Hyde, Andy Pogson, John Cleland, Gemma James-Smith, Jani Lauzon, Cara Ricketts, Françoise Balthazar, Thom Allison, and Leah-Simone Bowen. Every reading of the play helped me immensely. I am forever in your debt.

To the production team of Travis Murphy, Deanna Choi, Ryan Howard Clement, Isidra Cruz, Eli Ham, and the cast of Peggy Coffey, James Downing, Deborah Drakeford, and Martin Julien. Everyone came together in a short amount of time and gave it their all. Miigwetch for all of your fantastic work.

To Yvette Nolan, whose mentorship, grace, and dramaturgical eye continue to support and nurture me. I cannot thank her enough for everything she does for me. No one listens better than she does.

To anyone I may have missed, please know that I am grateful for your help and support. To the Creator, to the ancestors whose shoulders I stand on, and to those who will come after us, I honour you in this work. Chi Meegwetch.

Keith Barker is a Métis artist from Northwestern Ontario. A graduate of the George Brown Theatre School, he has worked professionally as an actor, playwright, and director for the past sixteen years. He is a recipient of the SATAward for Excellence in Playwriting and the Yukon Arts Audience Award for Best Art for Social Change for his play *The Hours That Remain*. He has served as a theatre program officer at the Canada Council for the Arts, and is currently the artistic director of Native Earth Performing Arts in Toronto.

First edition: October 2017. Second printing: August 2020.
Printed and bound in Canada by Marquis Imprimeur, Montreal.

Cover art and design by Travis Murphy
Author photo © Christian Lloyd

**PLAYWRIGHTS
CANADA PRESS**

202-269 Richmond St. W.
Toronto, ON
M5V 1X1

416.703.0013
info@playwrightscanada.com
www.playwrightscanada.com
@playcanpress

MIX
Paper from
responsible sources
FSC® C103567